THE PORTAGE POETRY SERIES

SERIES TITLES

The Walk to Cefalù
Lynne Viti

The Found Object Imagines a Life: New and Selected Poems
Mary Catherine Harper

Naming the Ghost
Emily Hockaday

Mourning
Dokubo Melford Goodhead

Messengers of the Gods: New and Selected Poems
Kathryn Gahl

After the 8-Ball
Colleen Alles

Careful Cartography
Devon Bohm

Broken On the Wheel
Barbara Costas-Biggs

Sparks and Disperses
Cathleen Cohen

Holding My Selves Together: New and Selected Poems
Margaret Rozga

Lost and Found Departments
Heather Dubrow

Marginal Notes
Alfonso Brezmes

The Almost-Children
Cassondra Windwalker

Meditations of a Beast
Kristine Ong Muslim

Steelhead

"A wonderful tension rides along with the current of each poem in this lovely book—the rift between reality and passion, the pang between an earlier, freer life and a more mature one, and the temptation that floods the distance between doubt and faith. At no point in the book does the poet seek to resolve these rich and persuasive tensions, and that tells me we're in the life-giving province of art. This is a deeply satisfying book to read, filled to the brim with spot-on imagery and set adrift with well-timed phrasing and lines and sudden pauses that make the entire flow come alive with love and candor."

—MAURICE MANNING
author of *The Common Man*
Pulitzer Prize Finalist

"*Steelhead*, Lauren K. Carlson's remarkable debut collection, is a Niedeckerian paean to place, shaped by the waters and winters of the rural Upper Midwest. In their explorations of isolation, family, faith, and the dynamic cross-currents between the natural world and the creative mind, these brilliant poems chart the dovetailings and divergences of 'life lived/and the life within' with fierce imagination and grace."

—DEBRA ALLBERY
author of *Fimbul-Winter*

"Like a fish-ladder allowing the Steelhead to leap falling water, poet Lauren K. Carlson runs language with and against, from observation to revelation. Rooted in the natural world and with great respect for our finitude, these gorgeous poems roam 'between the life lived/and the live within.' Formally inventive, rich, utterly alive. *Steelhead* is a magnificent debut, a collection of poems as ferocious as it is patient and wise. I want to know the world Carlson knows."

—SALLY KEITH
author of *Two of Everything*

STEELHEAD

poems

Lauren K. Carlson

CORNERSTONE PRESS
UNIVERSITY OF WISCONSIN-STEVENS POINT

Cornerstone Press, Stevens Point, Wisconsin 54481
Copyright © 2025 Lauren K. Carlson

www.uwsp.edu/cornerstone

Printed in the United States of America by
Point Print and Design Studio, Stevens Point, Wisconsin

Library of Congress Control Number: 2025931780
ISBN: 978-1-960329-66-0

Cornerstone Press titles are produced in courses and internships offered by the
Department of English at the University of Wisconsin–Stevens Point.

DIRECTOR & PUBLISHER
Dr. Ross K. Tangedal

EXECUTIVE EDITORS
Jeff Snowbarger, Freesia McKee

EDITORIAL DIRECTOR
Ellie Atkinson

SENIOR EDITORS
Brett Hill, Grace Dahl

PRESS STAFF
Cora Bender, Sophie McPherson, Kylie Newton, Ava Willett

for Saara

ALSO BY LAUREN K. CARLSON:

Animals I Have Killed

POEMS

I. [A Body Like Mine]

II. [Strength To Return]

III. [This Which Is Taking Shape]

ANATOMY OF A SEED

Relax, no one's extraordinary.
You can put down that full pail.
No more balancing, only surrender.
Let the bucket slosh, let water.

All that's asked of you, taste what's sweetest.
Sugar gives itself over to mouth.
Inside your throat's slick opening, flood.
Like unto a small animal's sacred cache, seasons break you—

And you open, primary root.
Radicle, yielding to the dark tunnels of your growth.

"we see what we sow, but not what we shall reap"

—*Norwegian Proverb*

"No, all this is not happening in real facts but rather in the domain of...of an art? Yes, of an artifice through which there arises a very delicate reality that comes to exist within me: that transfiguration has happened to me."

—Clarice Lispector, *Água Viva*

I. [A Body Like Mine]

PERENNIAL

North shore,
I pray out loud too.

As dune grasses pray—*Sleeping Bear*—
with their empty, crisp, quivers.

I'm bound, like anything else here,
alive in winter, to attempt survival.

Torn stem. Berries. Gull prints
lonesome for life's evidence.

Sunlight pools, wilts leftover snow and
where sand shifts ground, I imagine

warm pockets. Contained. Underneath,
new sacs heed nothing, not even cold.

AUBADE

Between the seeming moment
unending and the moment my three
finite children are born.

Within the unending moment each
child took to be
born and the seeming finite —now.

The first time,
the seeming moment teeming,
they, all three,

the bus to school together ride—
the five-year-old waves *goodbye*
and I watch them, in seconds,

seconds, go away. Seconds,
I swear, that's all it takes
for today

to ascend. Today like
a lover whom commitments forbid.
Forgive me, lover my commitments—

I was with.
Another way to put it is
between the life she lived,

and the life within
her: resistance.
Among the life you live,

and the life within
you reader: distance.
How long until you find

yourself all kitchen sink
and no choices.
Dust, dog-hair, crumbs,

stale fruits and last
labors, you.
The life within,

the life I bide abiding,
a lover,
like a forbidden lover,

like first love—
I followed them.
To where red wing blackbirds

rattled at the water's edge.
            River—there where we leapt, still water.
Life rinsing new fruit in cold water.

A red apple in the crisp cool.
The boathouse near the road.
And what fluttered through

the aspen's papered branches?
Red wing boundary between tree
line and sky, lift.

Black birds,
ink-edged border
between ground and high,

how it was impossible
to discern one bird
from another and how

those red fires rise—
        here
there's no distance

between one bird
            and the other bird.
Is commitment formation

or complacency? Flock—
and the crackles of leaves,
the snap of clean

apples and teeth,
between the life lived
and the life within,

the fire rising and
the night's descent.
            Who took the apples?

Where did they roll?
Where does ambition go?
Turn off the faucet,

mother—
The sink, the sink,
the water runs over.

YOU APPEAR TO BE ONLY A NAME

When it's never severed
gold stretches.

Therefore, if, as Frost asserts
gold is nature's hardest

hue to hold
perhaps he should consider

this a matter of physics.
Grasp whisps.

Evidenced by the slightest
remnant vein, love

an elemental, irreducible
gold unnamed.

What's weightless
will not fray.

ON MOTHER'S DAY

my son tries to break an egg
he grips it in his fist
as though he could squeeze it open

    but finding the egg
    resistant to even-sided pressures

he strikes
the roundest end against
the counter's edge
with force

    the resulting cracks
    grant his small hand
    a crushing power

membranes burst
past shattered shell-white

yolk bleeds down
his arm

    his face grows like a plant
    toward light

"See?"

    As if he broke sunshine
    over every valley on earth

As if he brought morning
to his mother in a silver bowl

DAWN ON THE 45TH PARALLEL

Daybreak makes
me see three-
dimensions flat.

I see black
paper instead
of poplars.

The world
a child's cut-out
scrap. My son

and I cast long
shadows, featureless
matte.

Light breaks
the same way
waters carve clay:

shifting what it kisses—
Unbidden creatures
diffuse through

wetland's sloughs
as what's hidden
becomes immediate.

Leopard frog, muskrat,
great heron,
blue.

SUMMER SOLSTICE IN LAC QUI PARLE

Now, at sunset, the children's
faces part the light
and take on darkened

cloaks, so for a moment, though
prairie wind animates brush
and crests its grasses, while tractors

roar through the fields, dust
hovering like holy ghost
over the surface of the shivering deep

loam as controlled burns
singe the invading sunflower edge
and we protect our uniform crop,

everything is foreshadowed
with reflexive clarity. The old ground
will crumble under cull and engine.

Rise and make cloudless a red
stinging sky. What would it mean to unimagine?
Unimagine, no, not being, but desire—

Unimagined desire, conduit to dissatisfaction,
what else is life?

[LITTLE MOON SONNET]

—for headwaters

Tile the fields. Lay pipe, make underground
waterways. Minimize flood, fertilize and
when torrents come, algae blooms
thick in the Lac qui Parle. All the Mississippi's
headwaters are green and I drive wherever
I like with a loud radio, no one can stop me—
All the Mississippi River's headwaters enriched
but I eat meat, corn-fed beef. I don't consider
cost. Wait. I do consider cost. Cheaper but worth it, that's worse—
Drain you away and fast. Yes, but you algae my rivers,
every night you little moon, you drag me along.
Not over this earth, but someplace like it. You go down.
Not over my body, but a body *like mine.*

INCARNATE

Your boundary
is the stitch-

ful of nothing.
Skin like sky

—two sides.
Horizon line—

your flesh, mine.
Mutuality's edge.

DRIVING HIGHWAY 67 WHILE LISTENING TO THIS AMERICAN LIFE

and the host to my horror describes
what happens when
a human heart gets left behind
                  in or on the airplane transporting it,

                  no that's not the whole story

though there are those who'd chalk-it-up to
                  life, luck, divine negligence, devil's curses, fate,
                  mad science, hot-button
medicine,

for all the ways
                  compatibility makes itself known
this curious reporter persists in search of:
                  How often,
                  how many? Forgotten hearts.
        Half miracles.
One in another's—
                  one loss puts off another's—

The radio host, from where? who knows—
                  likely some metropolis with a brick
                  and square, soundproof room
broadcasting unlikely complications
born of ingenuity and negligence;
                  which are [both]
                  human, [and] inhumane.

Aren't you and I each other's stewards?
Through any magnetic field,

radio waves rippling.
We cavity-carrying vessels.

Transplant patient, hurried attendant,   skillful pilot,
plane with failing engine,   our runway

—dear god—

intended solely for crop-dusters.

A MATTER OF DEGREES

How much I want to be good. The care with which I cut
apart rings sold with six packs of Diet Coke. Nonetheless, how

my ancient aluminum motorboat sinks in the lake. Takes on more disaster
than I can bail. How the water rises within until the boat's rim

forms a silver lip and the sinking like a throat's darkness. Gentle swallow.
My mother laying my brother to sleep in his crib, gentle like that. From shore,

someone watching. I remember I wave and I want. Not with my head
above water, something else. My voice sharing this story with you.

Is it too late? When goodness subsumes, what will I wave? A charged wire,
a tentacle, a net, a gun? Maybe to cooperate, they're too far gone.

This person and me. This person and you.
This person and the person near them, near us.

WHEEL

Not the blue
of a storm, not the absence of blue,
not blue's opposite which is fire, the dimpled
skin of an orange, acid, the blood moon, the bright irons
juxtaposed to midnight's calm, heavy blanketed, lightning
as the spectacle-delight to thunder's blues, as sea swells,
as prayers, the mind's ear, the spirit's tongue, multilingual,
the dove's descent, tinged with neon pink rage, rage, the
heart, blue muscle, red blood, all the visions which can't
be analyzed, everything witnessed unspoken, magenta
alongside the oblivions deep black-blue ringing the rim
of my life, eager the salt I gulped, ice, pale blue's
sudden intoxicant, sky-blue, truth rimming
stupor, purple's precedent,
steeled.

NARROW FELLOW IN THE GRASS

Confidence looks strange on a woman/ like a boa constrictor/ in the swamps of South America I saw one in a cage/ I did not shiver/ at the snake/ no narrow fellow was he/ but girthed like me/ round patterned flickering thing/ tone/ twisting into yet another/ spiral/ yet another/ strange tail extending/ that's me/ road-show-zoo-circus-beast/ again/ like me/ unusual isn't it/ most of the books I read/ the man is always older/ I tell you he thinks he is/ but never is/ older than me/ little girl the old woman said but I am/ little no longer/ I'm a boa'd thing/ scarf you'd hang with/ I guarantee/ nobody believes my age when I say it/ nobody believes how old / I am you see/ they say/ no way/ you are so beautiful/ they say it to my face/ a waste a beauty like that/ at her age/ heaven forbid/ I'm sure you've heard the story/ I was once a snake/ with legs/

LORD MAKE ME A RIVER

Lord, bring the pilgrim to me.

Lord, let him remove his shoes
and take off his hat near the boathouse

at my mouth. Lord, let her
wear a handmade dress or no dress at all.

Lord, would I say man— Lord, would I say woman—
Lord, would I say child. Put your feet in my water.

Lord, rub their callouses with my soft slick hands.
Rinse hair as they swim in me, their limbs spreading like leaves

most autumns on forest paths: fluttering, vivid, fallen.
Let my pockets of cold hold, O Lord.

You know the places where hurt brings heat.
Let them be soothed.

Lord, make me your first sign,
make me the last wine,

let the pilgrims taste and burst.
Let me under their skin.

II. [Strength To Return]

IMPATIENS

October, the south wind came, in force
out of season, and disruptive. The intrusion

kept alive what should not have been kept. Impatiens.
Should have been season of cold. Instead,

south wind's gales against everything. Against
branches, gates, sails. In the freshwater

sea there were waves, now breaking against opposing waves.
The surf the south brings. Humidity delights

what will ultimately suffer the hard freeze. Impatiens.
The riptide will pull you away from shore,

and no one is strong enough to overcome its current.
Swim out and not against. Swim out, then back toward shore.

In other words, once you've relented, you've got strength
to return. The seed pouch bursts when touched—the slightest touch.

PROVIDENCE TOWNSHIP

Imagine a night that's pure dark, where there are stars
merely sometimes and no illuminated roads home.

Picture the remarkable absence of artificial light.
Half asleep, you think you'd left a lamp on or worse,

didn't blow out the sagging candle in the dining room
before you headed to bed, only to finally figure

out the flickering is the curtain casting shadows, furnace air
hushing up from the heat register below, and the lace

blocks out moonlight coming through the window.
Outside November leaves circle December's surface, snow

and, like a gray steeple against a grayer night, still,
still the way a magnifying glass with its lens condenses

heat, a snowy owl. For the white winter hare, for you
this scene invites, not peace

        disease—

THEY CALLED IT GOOD FRUIT
[take and eat]

You can't stop
tasting this question

let it be
known you relish

let it be
known you detest

you who knows
love also knows

love's opposite
pacing

gravel feet crunching
pea rock all day

gnaw you at
bright nectar

and wonder
kiss or pucker

is it this way
a tart mouth

seethes unseen
juices

    which is

vinegar

    which is

wine

NOCTURNE AS SUPPLICATION

That night we ritualized our trespassing of time
by wandering the glossy lamp-lit streets at dark

naming each thing as though discovery and invention
belonged to us. We carried the same sinking one finds

in the bottom of a bag full of apples. A sweet
forbidden heaviness. How did we move?

We held the fruit in our hands.
We spread our fingers around it.

We pressed the cool skin against
one another's faces. We did not bite.

Hunger filled me.

THE LESSON

Last summer you taught my son to carve a spoon.
He asked, "Granddad, does wood bleed?"
For the way you didn't panic, thanks.
Answered, "No, but you do" and explained,
"The knife can be too sharp to feel it,"
held my son's bleeding palm in your hand,
told him to think each move before he moved it,
to check his small fingers, the blank,
his round leg where the blank rests and breathe—
I know you meant the lesson for my son.
Dad, the world is too sharp for me to feel it.
Teach me to strike deep with the *tollekniv*
until I find the soft wood under the birch bark,
to push away from the hand. Tell me to check my heart,
chest where the heart rests and breathe.
Say no hurry, say be silent.
And together we'll stay by the campfire
while jay birds call in the maple trees.
Then, when I am calm, I'll remember
to pay attention that I may feel the wound—
        the scarred hand carves a good spoon.

THE FLOWER GARLAND

I watch my niece
        decapitate
daisies in her backyard,
layered with last autumn's overgrown herbs and their silver sponge-rot
carpeting what once was lawn.

I don't think my brother's ex-wife
knew annual from perennial, how fast mint sends its roots
out into neighboring earth, to bloom again and again.

My mother keeps calling it my brother's fresh start,
but the words must wound my niece—
As though separation could till her mother into

rich soil. As though it were no violence
to harrow ground
and lay down something

sweet and fresh. As if longing
could be plucked, strung,
worn as adornment.

WINTER SOLSTICE

The deflated balloon of her skin
slung low under the jawbone

after her quadruplets were born;
we gave her red cell, grain

buckets, fresh water.
          Queenie recovered, brayed in the

pasture, played with her kids,
nestled in straw to sleep.

          She willfully submitted to the tugs
          and pats of young children.

But on the darkest day of the year,
she collapsed.

I have come to believe our goat died
not from pregnancy, its subsequent anemia,

but from winter.
          Winter and its violent lack.

          I whisper prayers to my son as we
          watch my husband pile

          smiling Amazon boxes on top her
          cold body. We watch a red

tongue of fire mouth the pyre.
Chickens huddle.

Among snow covered
                fields, tomorrow's ash heap

will be rare offering—
        Chickens won't know this

                dirt comes from burning
                dead. They'll burrow

blessing,
cluck celebration,
                fluff feathers.

Like strange winter flowers
they'll blossom from dust.

WATERSHED

—"How then were your eyes opened?" they asked.
John 9:10

There were no other
      homes where we lived.
            Our house faced a graveyard

surrounded by a grove
      our goats mowed down.
            Boer goats whose brays visitors

would mistake for children,
      hidden, crying out to be found.
            Boer goats with their pupils

like plats cut into planes.
      Dawn light made wheat
            appear as though it hovered over

swampy ditches. We squinted.
      Air a drum. Humid, round.
            Wind wilting grasses, blue stem,

locust song textured,
      sharp as fabric's static.
            Day charged grains

flood changed.
      Our walk to the bridge
            and back. At least five bald eagles

dove for grass carp
      caught where floodwater festered.
            Grass carp who'd followed one

another in snaking schools upstream.
Highwaters, algae-rich, threaded
severed wetlands. The fish now trapped—

Standing pools, stagnant water. Carp
rippled. Doomed, they circled.
Evaporating floodwater

left no tributary, no return.
Eagles tore into exhausted fish.
Scales glittered. Guts and odor.

Near the bridge we noticed something.
A new boulder? Or an old stump?
Sediment oozed around it, north bank

receding back to the place
where the water's rush met bridge
and drowned the black calf under.

We noticed weedy mats mucked
like caked blood. Sky clear
and wide.

Land burst like
an eye's darkened
bruise. Lid swollen shut.

STEER SKULL ON THE MINNESOTA-

South Dakota border.
Brown mule stirs up
dust, leopard frogs

disrupt blue stem.
Cicadas, their long songs,
comfort, hush and

darken the wind-broken
groves. We walk
the deer path

along the ditch side,
dusk. Stems of wheat
bow. The white-tail doe

shimmers through reverent
cornrows. A dull breeze, too
sidles. Evening after

our large dinner,
beef roast courtesy of our neighbor's
cow and we are full

neighboring, shy.
Neighboring and ashamed.
People sick and dying all around

our hillside, beef and town.
Here, where we walk, we believe
provision would be simple.

Imagine
how simple provision
would be.

ANIMALS I HAVE KILLED (running list)

the fox that ate our chickens   bullet & rifle & didn't
run   under the woodshed   woodchuck   rifle
& ran   two raccoons & shot through the soffiting
rifle again   but first tried to trap   chicken the dog
injured but didn't kill   bare hands & neck snapped   our
dog   she slipped under the front wheel of our truck
impact   do the goats we take to the butcher count
slaughtered   pheasants so many   I don't keep
track   hunted & stewed   deer   deer season   hunted
& shot   processed & ground & sausage & jerky
mounted   the skunk when we got home from Dairy
Queen   rifle again & didn't run again   a kitten   car
again   impact again & also crushed & I imagined
it was only sleeping   a bat smacked tennis racket but
meant it   soft   the rooster   burned alive for
attacking my son   farm I confess   I find no peace
for wild things   why   God spoke
breath & dust   chaos & light of thousands   suns
am I steward   dare he call me

                    beloved

VOW

Outside. Outside the April blizzard rages.
Inside the house, our lights all quiver. But
quivers are for arrows. Inside, our lights flicker.

Our lamps are lit. Wind shakes our panes. Until
we lose our power and the lamps go out. Let's
when the lights flicker, quiver. Who knows

sublimation like longtime lovers? The heart
longs for rattling walls. The heart: stuck full
of arrows. I forgot how loud blizzards sound,

and their dim illumination which is candles
in the power outage dark. Late winter roaring,
but the roar my own. The quaking, my own wall

and rattled heart. On and off, expand
contract the longing, linger. Let's when dawn,
when discovery suns our human risk,

wake up humming with our hands full of dew
jewels uncovered from our field. Grasp clippings.
Their emerald glow let's envision. As though ground,

that hidden treasure under ice, that glimmer
emerging between striations of rock and snow
now bladed small gems saturate.

Seasons change because the earth moves.
Like when I saw fire, and before fire,
the crackling. Before crackling, billows

standing in air, the scent: char, spearmint, and meat.
The gray-white fog that veiled.
The smoke which promised heat.

INVASIVES

Burdock will catch your thigh,
hook the eye of your cotton weave,

between two threads—eye. There
is the open place. Where burr sticks

any soft, vulnerable, membrane—please.
Please hear me. I am inexperienced.

Any fecund field is haunt. All through me.
A sun ray fell across my shoulder. With a clang.

Hairs on my shoulders stand erect, hackles erect.
My bones a singed wick and my muscle, my skin: flames.

There's a mean sun. Daylight has many expectations.
I resist measurement. On the other hand

am impatient for forward progress, fruitful
change. I've lived seconds in the first year of my infant life.

I've been a thousand years inside one day of grief.
How long will it take, to clear the grove of these seeds?

MERCY SEAT

The same blood
the butcher drains
when he strings
the bull upside-down
with a chain

is the honey
I gathered the day
I straddled the branch
and punctured the hive
with a needle.

You, too, must live
within the gaping
wound you'll become,
offering what
you once protected

to be slaughtered.
During the season
of falling honeybees
whose wing-flash and fury

blur leaf bud with sound,
I give thanks for this,
the sting of iron

on my lips.

AMPHIBIAN

—after Denise Levertov

Others prayed as if prayers
were wishes. But I'd
blow out candles before
the song finished.
I learned to plug my nose
and dive, to glide unseen
upstream with trout,
and make my home among
clusters of egg sac,
stream disturbed with rock
and stem. There, in the ceaseless
whisper of living water, breath
brought me out from under
the lilies. I was cold, struggling.
Sharp light devoured
my gills, but the brook bubbled
and the steelhead spawned.
Nothing was longing,
except I:
        woman living
        two worlds

III. [This Which Is Taking Shape]

DEFT COMPARISONS

blossom	process	(over time opens)
sprout	produce	(fruiting body)
disruption	crack	(life needs to hatch)
ripe	artifice	(heightens sense)
fortune	rot	(germinates)
plum[b]	word	(cuts teeth)

FEAST OF

anger, like you can sink teeth into, candy apple,
like one part indulgent and two-part sour,
like certain to spoil if left out,
like to the core—impaled,
like hand-held,
like admirable under cellophane,
like wish you had sweet, wish you didn't have sticky,
like leave its glaze on everything,
like how hard and good it is to make clean,
like that pure green-skin fruit,
like whole, underneath—

CAST-OFF

Love like pine sap.
Sticky in the wrong places.
Bob Daniels sold his family
home in Manistee,
guess you never know
what'll bend someone's nose.
We could save humanity
if we evaporated humans.
The bearded iris bloomed today.
How dare she—doesn't she know
we're suffering? Selfish flower
whose true age is uncertainty,
Mr. Daniels never sold
his home to anyone.
To unlock my ancient parts
I camped for a week
at the bottom of Lake Michigan.
I breathed such freshwater.
I never told how.
Unreal fabric, sea floor,
which swaddles all of us:
jeweled maggots. If only we knew
ourselves grub and wholly.
Like ruby-throated wings,
the clear water of time humming.
Hands at the wheel, teenage girl.
We all *wanna dance with somebody*.

LOCATION HISTORY

Near rivers.
Near creaks.
Near gutters.
Near storm drains.
Near dams.
Near fish ladders.
Near faucets.
Near shower heads.
Near wells.
Near ponds.
Near sloughs.
Near the artesian spring.
Near rainfall.
Near snow showers.
Near thunderstorms.
Near oceans.

Always along
the waterways,

where is the water
I know, I know well its shores—

God must not exist
us so close to heavens.

So distant, deserted
from the paths

called water,
God must not.

STEELHEAD

A rainbow trout that has migrated from its stream habitat into the Great Lakes is called a steelhead. These develop into silver fish with a steely blue head and back.

St. Ignatius defined suffering as desire
disordered. The city of Grand Rapids

fluoridated its water June 25,
1945, to avoid needless suffering—

and since observing the plaque at the monument
Steel Water I've been wondering what exactly,

is needful suffering? When I tell folks
about how I broke all my front teeth

during first grade recess people ask, yes but
were they permanent? Which I took to mean

my loss was a painless loss thanks to baby teeth's
planned obsolescence. Though it hurt so bad

I quake in my sleep to this day from the pain.
A life of my own, with you there too. Side by side

La-Z-Boys, Christmas each week. Backyard with woods
and a creek. Ian Curtis says people in this world have no place

to go—*Up, down, turn around.* Ignatian spiritual practices
consist of identifying false consolation, hard consolation.

In 1988 I first observed love indistinguishable from explosive
effort. The trout jumping the ladder: hard consolation.

Swimming against grief, the fish leapt falling water.
Damming the river, enough hydroelectricity to reorder want.

Rainbow trout return home to spawn. Attachment tears us
apart again. The fish-ladder is functional artwork, concrete

sculpture allows spawning fish ability to circumvent
the 6th St Dam. A barrier only the strongest steelhead

were capable of leaping (at least it wasn't my young heart).
Say it's the last time. The great body came first.

Then tributaries.

THE PHOTOGRAPH HOLDS
IN CONTRAST

night tree rough bark soft light feathery and welcoming
and then we were walking the deer was not
      one leg missing or was one leg hurt and held higher than the rest

I couldn't tell or could tell then but can't tell you now the point
the gait was uneasy had an uneasy gait

I an uneasy gate opening closing opening closing
next to you meadow across from which was the cemetery
graves in Swedish how lilacs extending delicate fingers
could I photograph this shadow foolish thought but
      the shadow followed

you were a runner once you said
high elevation made your lungs strong
Roger Bannister broke the impossible
      but I was that three-legged

deer how appropriate I have extraordinary attributes
for instance, once I purchased Eileen Fisher pants for twenty-five-cents
believe it or not I won't say if you won't   best pair
there where the streetlight keeps going off and on for some reason
      cicadas dropping like stars dropping like stars
      is what I would say but stars don't drop
      they shoot

who hasn't seen them in the forest or some remote lakeshore
but I mean falling really shooting like the plague whizzing like hail
like sudden midsummer thunderstorm
rattling wings getting stuck in my hair what I mean is
      oh man photographs take me back

can you tell I'm desperate for attention and worse than your worst enemy
I mean ordinary monotonous boring amusement

hold it up for the phone just like that
promise hope to die cross the dock the blue fish bit
did you catch one how fitting
          the snagged hook in the belly at the end of the line

THE GROUND IS NOT DOWN

There was someone
in girlhood I loved.

It was easy, like not giving up.
I didn't even need

to try. All I needed
was to not stop

until I was dead.
Staying isn't the same

as striving. It's yielding
as a body must yield

under gravity. Like how up
and down aren't rendered

by human perception.
They're rendered by force.

How the earth's center
pulls everything toward it.

How a bridge's supports
pitch to account for earth's curve.

How the earth bids all things
made or born

surrender,
surrender.

AFTER THE DANCING

came the beloved feeling—making
itself at home. An old good dog

going round in circles twice
before settling down. After the dancing,

all over your skin thin crystals, salt.
All sour, glimmer, shine. After the dancing

and warm. In its sleep that dog
whines, chases after the dancing

the way your heart longs for someplace it can't.
You're going home after the dancing.

You're on an empty street. The streetlight's
orange and flashing after the dancing.

Somewhere inside a wire's come loose,
you're saying goodbye after the dancing.

It's time. Some dog out there's living
the heart's best life: after the dancing,

sleep and freedom. How a bed makes
hair look wet, after the dancing.

It's morning but not
a new day yet, after the dancing

Your heart, rewinding and
replaying each scene after the dancing,

Trying to find a way to talk, hear.
How folks repeat sorry for your loss after the dancing.

There, drifting in spirit like water,
water the deep color of April violets after the dancing.

A spirit like March in Michigan gathers ice
and life after the dancing.

The strong current pulling you back
together after the dancing,

galaxies bubbling. A whirlpool center,
out and away. After the dancing.

She didn't know it was her last
good time. After the dancing

each one cast onto opposing
rocky banks. Sharp stones.

MAKING UP AFTER AN ARGUMENT

look
how the strange
boned body

flexes
in the slough
at you

weak
observer
the vision

not the wing
illusive
though near

anhinga's feathers want water
and as they dive— dive
spread absorb

meantime
light-numbed
birders trot

the dock
slow in circled
binoculars

water lily's
broad leaves
dart open

tease our curled fins
and sun stung
eyes

UNTO OTHERS

In the forest I toured the wildflowers,
at home destroyed dandelions.

In my heart I praised original thought,
among the crowds conformity.

I petitioned the counselors to listen,
hoping to overhear myself.

To my friends I claimed the book was better,
but watched the film alone and wept.

Night fell and I joined the plunderers,
yet woke defending my riches.

In the congregation I rejected authority,
among peers followed their precepts.

With my prayers I begged for God to act.
As for my life, I was sovereign.

CLOCK TIME vs FELT TIME

I'm wondering why I went so long without—

but waiting is also a way to measure
and measurement turns imagined realities, such as time,

> because it's true isn't it,
> that time is perception, mostly,
> sensible through light and motion, cosmic, planetary
> some combination of belief and matter, much like faith,

into blocks
that is the hours, they are comprised of minutes broken into seconds,
which aren't broken at all, until they're notched by the clock's
hands and then struck, the striking is what marks them, these blocks
called time

—why I went so long with comfort.

*

I devoted myself to deprivation. Suffering I marked, deprivation
    like a clock hand.
That consistent ticking. A shelter.

Its repetitions. A shelter.

My small suffering a purposeful—punishment?

No, a discipline and these mimic one another. Not punitive.
Rather, out of my endurance arrived a habit.

How much like a blanket, covering.

PRAYER

Heaven, please be a grand table.
Scent of pot roast means *honey set yourself down.*
Heaven, please meet my appetites, the deepest
kinds, peace thirst and justice hunger.
And the glasses toasting like windchimes
rising and falling with all the eaters'
gusts of laughter, gale force laments
breezy pleasure, steadfast anger.
Heaven let me get up stuffed. And still
served dessert. Cheeze Kurls and Better-Made
BBQ Chips and dip during the game.
Heaven, Vernors and RC, leftover roast beef
sandwiches buttered and mayonnaised.
Heaven, extra salt. Until I can't chew
another bite. Hands that won't clean till morning.
Dishes stacked, heaven, in the sink overnight.

ANGLING

—*What I am seeking is not here, and for that very reason I believe it.*
Søren Kierkegaard

Were the hook yanked out
though you're not supposed to

tear an opening in the filament.
The dark line of your lamellae

a boiled red rope, the flesh a curtain.
A red current, the cup inside you tipped.

You're supposed to be whole
with its—the river's—potions.

Instead, you've torn into an emptiness,
the ribcage around the heart's chambers

like potter's hands, caressing both
what was and isn't yet—

After the hook finds the gill
after the potter throws the clay

you're supposed to wait,
you're supposed to be filled.

But what's breath without emptiness,
potential without material.

The cup absent thirst,
form without scale.

TO BE A BETTER LISTENER

Night's pitch
thrown through
the eardrum, blue
but deeper than
blue. Dark like great
waters when calm
are flat or glass
seen into and through,
surface and depth.
The ancients perceived
two dreams: the waters above
and the waters below,
which reality parses.
The body real
as a knife
through fruit.

FIRST MIRACLE

Tupperware, stoneware, glassware, wood-carved,
porcelain, copper, red-solo, handmade, homemade,
factory-made, store-bought, collected, passed down,
thrifted. Wasn't that what the glasses were made for,
for holding? How many things had she put her mouth
around to stay alive? And why did this make the gesture—
how her lover cupped both hands in the freshwater stream
bubbling out of the earth, and offered them to her lips
to drink—why did her lover's hands, offered to her mouth
as a container, in whose placement she'd be restored,
feel like the one time she'd known ceaseless thirst?

MANIFESTO AGAINST
THE UNIVERSAL [[?]]

The world of the outer senses is the world/
The world of the inner senses is the world/

And do I consent to the peonies, reaching?
And do I consent to the tulip's bleeding petals?
And do I consent to the narcissus who declines to raise her face?
And do I consent to the maple who lords all?

And I consent to your hand,
which reaches inside me.

And I consent to your warmth
where my skin enters your mouth.

And I consent to my physical body
which cannot become your body.

And I consent to the pleasure of meeting
our separate bodies with intimacy—

* * *

There is no intimacy without distance,

No distance without synapse. No thought
without the space across which this nerve grasps.

no world without consent to the world.

DEFT CORRESPONDENCES

shoe: horse
stone: old
last: long
won: cow
wine: cloud
sewn: wide

tree: root
path: fawn
friend: wrong
ring: hole
no: fate
torn: threat

star: shot
new: map
dish: glass
sing: hold
ex: earth
stitch: hum

RIPE ARTIFICE

I resent my aliveness in so far as it means
    an illusion of toward.

       As though time were a straight road. Point "A"
    to point "B" and
each day one walks further down the line. Road.
    What is point "B"

       but a drop-off, an oblivion? The time/line/road
    is one's own, sure,
but also belongs to the globe. Now imagine the earth
    as a bowling

       ball rolling toward point "B," the drop off.
I resist this framework. I feel it inaccurate.

       There are millions of pinheads. My life: a force
    which presses against
the pins, and so the artifice, the fabric comprised
    of many points,

       takes on a topography. This topography is shaped
    through increments called days.
The days form a life. The days then, when we mark
    them, do not

       march us forward toward oblivion. No.
    They take shape.
This is what I mean by life. A topography formed. This
which is
    taking shape.

Yes. And each of us who live shape it.
       Yes. Life does not arrive to us shapeless—

its contours continue.

NOTES

"You Appear To Be Only A Name" is taken from a line in Merwin's "To the Light Of September."

"Amphibian" owes a debt to the work of Denise Levertov.

ACKNOWLEDGMENTS

Abandon Journal, "Feast of"

Amethyst Review, "Perennial"

Bearings Online, "Winter Solstice" "Unto Others"

Blue Earth Review, "Anatomy of a Seed"

Crab Creek Review Poetry Prize Semi-finalist, "Aubade"

Fatal Flaw, "The Flower Garland"

Fiolet & Wing: A Fabulist Anthology, "Amphibian"

Inflectionist Review, "Location History"; "You Appear To Be Only A Name"; "Incarnation"; "Manifesto Against The Universal"; "Clock Time Versus Felt Time"; "The First Miracle" ; "Making Up After An Argument"

Laurel Review, "Driving Highway 67"

LEON Literary Review, "Summer Solstice in Lac Qui Parle"; "The Photograph Holds In Contrast"

Mudroom, "Vow"

Orison Books Poetry Prize Finalist, "Nocturne As Benediction"

Pirene's Fountain, "Providence" "Impatiens"

Quarter After Eight, "A Matter Of Degrees"

Rivermouth Review, "After The Dancing"

Salamander Magazine, "Kinesthesia"; "Steer Skull on the South Dakota"

The Shore, "How To Be A Better Listener"

Sweet: A Literary Confection, "Invasives"

Terrain, "Dawn on the 45th Parallel"; "The Ground Is Not Down"

Vita Poetica, "Prayer"

Waxwing, "Wrecked" ; "Ripe Artifice"

"Amphibian" "The Lesson" "Lord Make Me A River" "Nocturne As Benediction" and "Winter Solstice" appeared together in the chapbook collection *Animals I Have Killed*, winner of *Comstock Review*'s 2018 Chapbook Prize.

* * *

Thank you to Tin House Winter Workshop, the Warren Wilson MFA Program for Writers, Napa Valley Writers' Workshop, Sewanee Writers' Workshop, The Collegeville Institute, the Southwest Minnesota Arts Council, the Loft Literary Center and Friends of Writers for support and instruction.

I'll start, first and foremost, with a thank you for the gentle encouragement, careful attention, and wisdom granted me by the Cornerstone Press staff: Director & Publisher Dr. Ross Tangedal, Senior Editor Grace Dahl, editors Kylie Newton and Cora Bender, and Sophie McPherson, Ava Willett, and Zoie Dinehart with media and sales. How glad I am to have discovered this wonderful Midwest press through *Wisconsin People & Ideas* in Lorine Niedecker's home on Black Hawk Island—

I'm thankful to Saara Myrene Raappana, who welcomed me as a writer to Southwest Minnesota, who steered me in the direction of the Warren Wilson MFA Program for Writers, who supervised my chapbook, who encouraged and challenged me, and I'm deeply grieved I won't be able to share this collection with her—

To RG, AW, SK SB, DA, and MM, you were my guides—

To my MFA cohort and Warren Wilson colleagues including HK, RP, MdA, ED, DL, and EC—

To the editors and staff at TPJ—

To BS, EF, SMR, ED, MMZ, EB, LF, BG, EW, LT, GR, JSS, SC and the other artists, writers, people and friends I met on the prairie and lakeshore and everywhere in between—

To the candle-burners—

To EAJSR—

And to my family.

LAUREN K. CARLSON is a poet and spiritual director living in Manistee, Michigan. Her work has recently appeared in *Crab Creek Review, Salamander Magazine, Terrain, The Windhover* and *Waxwing*. In 2022, she won the Levis Stipend from Friends of Writers for her manuscript in progress. Her writing has been supported by Tin House, Napa Valley Writers' Conference, and Sewanee Writers' Conference. She currently serves as editor for *Tinderbox Poetry Journal* and holds an MFA in poetry from the Warren Wilson MFA Program for Writers.